QUICK STARTS
FOR YOUNG CHOIRS

Activities and Ideas to Focus Young Singers

By Cristi Cary Miller and Angela K. McKenna

CHAPTERS

T0084246

HAL•LEONARD®
CORPORATION

7777 W. BLUEMOUND RD. P.O. BOX 13819 MILWAUKEE, WI 53213

Visit Hal Leonard Online at
www.halleonard.com

Introduction

Teaching young singers and keeping them engaged during the learning process is a challenge that many music educators face. Because of this, they are constantly asking colleagues about techniques and ideas, attending workshops to learn more and reading everything they can find about this area of instruction. There is never too much information that can be gained!

As we began to develop this idea for a book, we knew we had a lot of things to share but, most certainly, they were not all of our own concepts. In fact, many of these presentations were either given to us by colleagues or developed from their ideas. Because of this, there are many we would like to recognize for giving us inspirations: Cheryl Lavender, Rebecca Lindley, Jan Smith, Marilyn Woods, Kathlyn Reynolds, Leslie Orvis, Ralph Duncan, Billie Thomas, Laura Bartlett, and Dr. Shermie Potts, just to name a few. There are also many of these items shared in this book that we do not know from whom or where they came. We just know we discovered them through our years of teaching and they work with our students.

Our hope is that you will find this book to assist you with new ideas or regenerate techniques you have forgotten about to help in making your music year more successful. Thank you for giving us an opportunity to become a part of your teaching world. Best wishes for your new year!

Angie McKenna and Cristi Cary Miller

Warm Ups:
MUSCLE MOVEMENT

Singers should never overlook the need to warm up their muscles, as the whole body should be ready and involved for good singing. These warm up ideas are sure to get your students' bodies engaged immediately in the singing process.

DOUBLE TIME

1. Have students stand and mirror an action that you hold in place for 8 counts. For example, extend and hold your right arm across and overhead, and count aloud to 8.

2. After 8 counts, switch to an opposite action (extend left arm across and overhead) and count aloud to 8.

3. Repeat both actions above for another set of 8 counts apiece. At the end of the last set of eight, say, "Double time, here we go!"

4. Perform the above actions, now counting to four. Repeat for 2 sets (16 beats) and then say, "Double time, here we go!"

5. Perform the above actions, now counting to 2. Repeat for 4 sets (16 beats) and then say, "Double time, here we go!

6. Finally, perform the actions, now counting "one" for 8 sets (16 beats).

7. The entire pattern looks like this:

Right arm	8 counts
Left arm	8 counts (2 sets)
Right arm	4 counts
Left arm	4 counts (2 sets)
Right arm	2 counts
Left arm	2 counts (4 sets)
Right arm	1 count
Left arm	1 count (8 sets)

Personal note: This activity is great for waking up your choir without them having to think. It can be done with a multitude of opposite body motions, i.e. reach high/reach low, shoulders up/shoulders down, reach across with right hand/reach across with left hand, etc. Be prepared for lots of giggles!

MIRROR ME

1. Have students stand, and explain to them about the image in a mirror.
2. Tell them you are the "real deal" and they are the mirrors.
3. Begin with simple movement. For example, slowly raise an arm into a stretch as students follow.
4. Add another simple movement. For example, slowly raise the other arm.
5. Continue adding more complex motions, i.e. cross legs, raise arms, tilt head, bend over, etc.
6. Enhance the activity by having students lead.

ADD SOME MUSIC, PLEASE

Materials
- Recorded music (or a good pianist!)

1. Play a recording of an upbeat song.
2. While listening, have singers follow you as you move various parts of your body. For example knee bends, arms moving up/down or in opposition, twist, toe touches, etc.
3. If the song allows, create motions representing: whole notes, half notes, quarter notes, etc. If using this method, tell them when your movement shows one note value movement and the next.

Extension
Consider using student leaders

....

Personal note: A favorite song of my students I use with this activity is the Celtic Woman's recording of "Orinoco Flow." This song allows the usage of the whole, half, quarter and eighth notes movements. Every year my women's chorus demands to do this warm up with this song. It's a winner!

....

BRAIN BUSTER

1. Have the singers stand and ask them to speak the alphabet as they snap their right hands, and count from 1 to 26 as they snap their left hands. They should do this in an alternating format, i.e. "A-1, B-2, C-3" etc.

2. On another day, have them switch the alphabet/counting to the opposite hands.

Personal note: Although the brain is not a muscle nor does it contain any, this is a wonderful way to wake up both hemispheres of your brain!

CLIMB UP THE LADDER

1. Ask your students to stand and pretend to climb up a ladder.

2. As they reach for each new rung on the ladder, have them hold on with one hand as they look down at the ground to see how far they've come.

3. Have them continue to climb with one hand and then the next, continuing to look down at various times.

Other Ideas

Have them climb a rope ladder; ask them to reach high upon a shelf to get the cookie jar down; reach with one arm and then the next to try and unlatch a door whose lock is out of reach; etc.

WALK COUNTDOWN

1. Have singers stand randomly around the room.

2. Play a drum to establish a tempo and ask singers to walk around the room to that beat while counting to eight.

3. Without stopping, have them repeat the process, but this time they will stop walking/counting aloud on "8" and clap instead.

4. Repeat the process again, this time leaving off both "7" and "8" and replacing them with claps.

5. Continue the pattern until all singers are standing in place clapping the 8 beats.

   The pattern will look like this:

   1 – 2 – 3 – 4 – 5 – 6 – 7 – 8

   1 – 2 – 3 – 4 – 5 – 6 – 7 *clap*

   1 – 2 – 3 – 4 – 5 – 6 *clap – clap*

   1 – 2 – 3 – 4 – 5 *clap – clap – clap* (etc.)

6. On another day, this activity can be reversed so that all begin clapping to "8," then walking on "1" and clapping to "7," walking on "1" and "2" and clapping to "6," etc.

Personal note: Musicians always need to be thinking ahead. This activity reinforces that skill.

SHOULDER RUB

1. Ask your singers to make a quarter turn to the right so they are facing the back of the neighbor to his/her right.

2. On your signal, have them give their neighbor a back massage by following these steps:

   • Rub shoulders

   • Lightly karate chop shoulders and down back

   • Finger poke shoulders and down spine

   • Scratch backs

   • Pat backs

3. Have students turn to the opposite neighbor and perform the same actions.

Personal note: My women's chorus likes to end this activity by giving each other a hug!

Warm Ups:
MOVEMENT AND SINGING

It's a great idea to warm up muscles and voices at the same time. Here are a few fun ideas that should do the trick.

HEAD, SHOULDERS, KNEES AND TOES

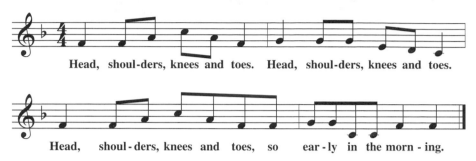

Head, shoul-ders, knees and toes. Head, shoul-ders, knees and toes.

Head, shoul-ders, knees and toes, so ear-ly in the morn-ing.

1. Have singers stand and ask them to touch the associated body part as they sing this song. (For "early in the morning," have them clap a quarter note beat.)

2. Repeat the song three more times, moving up the starting pitch by half steps. Each time begin the song with the next body part listed. For example, "Shoulders, knees, toes and head," then "Knees, toes, head and shoulders," and finally, "Toes, head shoulders, knees."

CHUMBARA

Chum-ba-ra, chum-ba-ra, chum-ba-ra, chum-ba-ra, chum-ba-ra, chum-ba-ra,

chum, chum, chum, chum, chum, chum, chum, chum. Chum! Chum! Chum!

1. Ask singers to stand. Teach this song by rote. Once learned, substitute in different 3-syllable words. For example, "merrily," "elephant," etc.

2. Ask students for other ideas, which can include words they know or even three different one syllable sounds, i.e. "Do" "key" "bah"

3. For added fun, have them perform the hand jive while singing.

DOOT, DOOT, DOOT

To the tune of "Good King Wenceslas"

1. Sing the song on "doot" for the choir. Then, teach the melody one phrase at a time.

2. When the group is comfortable with the tune, add the motions, having them echo sing/move one phrase at a time.

3. When the song and actions are learned, perform together.
   (This warm up can be done seated or standing. If seated, have students stand up and sit down on "the wave.")

4. Finally, sing the song as a 2- and/or 3-part round.

Personal note: Although this song works well during the holiday season, my students like performing it all year long.

DUM DITTY

Have students perform this warm up while sitting down.

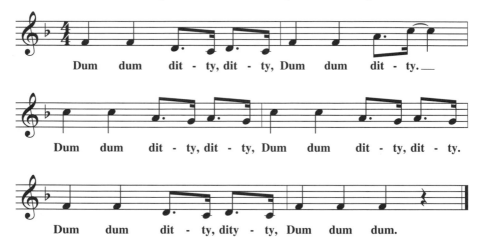

1. Sing the song for the choir and then teach them the melody, one phrase at a time.

2. When the song is learned, ask them to sing again, patting on the last three "dum, dum, dum's." Explain they will *always* pat on these words.

3. Now, teach the following patterns:

   • **Pattern 1:**

     ○ Pat legs (2 times)
     ○ Move hands to the right, patting your neighbor's leg with your R hand and your R leg w/your L hand (2 times)
     ○ Pat legs (2 times)
     ○ Move hands to the left, patting your neighbor's leg with your L hand and your L leg w/your R hand (2 times)

   • **Pattern 2:**

     ○ Pat legs (2 times)
     ○ Cross arms and pat legs (2 times)
     ○ Pat legs (2 times)
     ○ Reach arms out and pat both neighbor's legs to R/ L (2 times)

- **Pattern 3:**
  - ○ Extend R arm out, palm up, and w/L hand, tap R wrist (1 time)
  - ○ Tap R elbow joint (1 time)
  - ○ Cross arms, a la "I Dream of Jeanie" (1 time)
  - ○ Extend L arm out, palm up
    (Repeat the above 4-beat pattern using the opposite arms)
- **Pattern 4:**
  - ○ Pat legs (1 time)
  - ○ Touch L ear w/R hand as L hand touches nose (1 time)
  - ○ Pat legs (1 time)
  - ○ Touch R ear w/L hand as R hand touches nose (1 time)

4. When the patterns are learned, sing the song through 4 times, performing the patterns in sequence on each repeat. (Remember to have them pat on the "dum, dum, dum's" at the end of *each* pattern.)

5. Sing the song faster on each repeat.

Personal note: This warm up is by far one of my students' favorite!

CHOCOLATE COOKIE

(to the tune of "Sarasponda")

1. Sing the song to the class and then teach it to them, one phrase at a time.

2. When the song is learned, add the following cumulative actions to accompany the words. (One action is added on each repeat.)

- "chocolate" = clap twice
- "cookie" = snap once
- "yum, yum, yum" = rub belly three times
- "Oreo" = make a circle overhead with arms
- "I love that creamy filling" = jazz hands R/L/R/L
- "Hey" = punch R fist in the air

BEAT FUN

(with "Scotland's Burning")

This is a seated activity. Have students sit close enough together so that they can touch the singers to their right and left.

Scot-land's burn - ing. Scot-land's burn - ing.   Look   out! Look out!

Fi - re! Fi - re! Fi - re! Fi - re! Pour on   wa - ter. Pour on   wa - ter.

1. Sing through this song.

2. Review with the class the beat values for a whole note, half note, quarter note, and eighth note.

3. Teach the following pattern:

   • Pat your legs (1 time)

   • Move your hands to the R and pat this neighbor's L leg with your R hand as you pat your R leg with your L hand (1 time)

   • Pat your legs (1 time)

   • Move your hands to the L and pat this neighbor's R leg with your L hand as you pat your L leg with your R hand (1 time)

4. Once the pattern is learned, sing through the song as you perform the pattern, first using a whole note beat, followed by a half note beat, then a quarter note beat and finally an eighth note beat.

15

IF ALL THE LITTLE RAINDROPS

1. Have students stand and teach them this song.

2. As you speak the 1st verse instructions (measure 9), students echo while performing the action. They stay in this position and sing the song again.

3. On the second time through, repeat the 1st verse ("thumbs up") and then add the 2nd verse ("elbows in") with singers following the instructions. They sing the song in this position.

4. Continue adding a movement on each repeat.

Personal note: When students sing with head up and tongue out, you will notice there is an increase in volume. Reference this later when talking about vocal freedom!

MY BONNIE

1. Teach the song to the choir. (Be sure to explain what a "bonnie" is as many times they think you're singing "my body"!)

2. When the song is secure, ask the group what beginning consonant they hear the most. (B)

3. Have them sing again, snapping on each "B" word.

4. Now, explain they will stand/sit each time they sing a word beginning with the letter "b." For example, they will begin by sitting. When they sing the word "Bonnie," they stand and remain standing until they sing the next "Bonnie," which is when they will sit. They continue standing/sitting throughout the song.

5. For a fun alternative, divide the choir, having half start standing and the other half sitting.

MY BONNIE
Alternative Idea

To Prepare

Teach the song, "My Bonnie Lies Over the Ocean."
(See previous page) For each word, show the motions found below:

- "My" = point to self
- "Bonnie" = "jazz" hands on each side of face to represent pretty or handsome
- "lies" = hands like a prayer to side of head, head tilted, as if to sleep
- "over" = one hand in a fist and the other placed cupped over it
- "the" = *no movement for this word*
- "ocean" = move one hand like waves in front of body
- "sea" = form the alphabet letter C with hand
- "bring" = pretend to row a boat backwards
- "back" = touch your back
- "Oh" = make the letter "O" with fingers of both hands

1. Sing the song and add one motion at a time on each repeat.
2. Speed it up for added fun.

ZUMMA

Move up the scale by half steps.

Zum-ma, zum-ma, zum-ma-ma.   Zum-ma, zum-ma, zum-ma-ma.

Zum-ma, zum-ma, zum-ma-ma. Zum-ma, zum-ma, zum-ma-ma - ma.

1. After singers have learned the song, have them march in place, pumping their arms up and down in opposition.

2. At the end of each verse, move the pitch up/down by half steps, and have students make a ¼ turn to their right or left and repeat.

Extension

Have students think of other 2-syllable words that could be used to replace "zumma."

AROOSTASHA

1. Have singers stand to learn this warm up as they echo you in 2-measure phrases. Use a high pitched head voice as you demonstrate.

2. After students are familiar with the words, lead them through the actions as you state each one and they echo. For example, you say, "Thumbs up," and they echo. Then, you say, "Here we go!" and they echo.

3. This is a cumulative song. Each time you add a verse, you begin with the first verse and work your way down.

4. Encourage your singers to come up with additional verses that might be added.

Personal note: As silly as this warm up seems, all of my students seem to enjoy it. It also works great for warming up that head voice.

Warm Ups:
VOCAL

There are countless warm ups that work for singers. Sometimes we have the tendency to use the same ones over and over. Although this can be a good thing, occasionally, to keep singers interested, it's fun and important to use new ideas to keep their interest. Here are but a few more warm ups to add to your list of "must do's."

HOOTS AND HOLLERS

To Prepare

Practice on your own by making various 4-beat "hoots & hollers." For example:

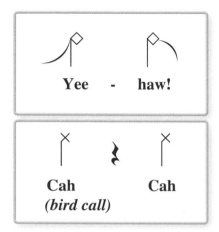

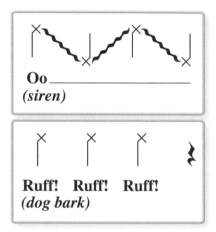

Other Ideas

- cat purr
- donkey bray
- tweets
- Sh – sh – sh (or any consonant)

1. Make a hoot or holler as students echo.
2. Continue the process as singers respond.

Personal note: This is great for an attention-getter. Simply practice with your students by having them talk among themselves. Tell them you will give them three "call and answers." After the third one, they need to be focused and ready to sing. Next, wait for them to get a little "into" their conversations. Then, do a series of three hoots and hollers. This will snap them back to attention in an instant.

WARMING UP
WITH THIS OLD MAN

To Prepare

Create cards with the following words written on them: "key," "did," "zoo," "pep," and "ma." Also, create a card with a fermata sign on it.

1. Hold up one of the word cards and ask your students to sing this word to the melody of "This Old Man."

2. Have them continue to sing as you change the word cards.

3. Randomly, pull up the fermata card. (This can happen in the middle or end of phrases.)

4. Sing the song, moving up by half steps, as you change the cards throughout.

Personal note: This idea can be used with any melody. During the holiday season, it's especially fun to use Christmas melodies.

WRITE YOUR NAME

1. Ask your singers to use their head voices as they write their names in the air.

2. Consider other words they can write in the air, i.e. school name, mascot, mother's name, etc.

B – A BAY

B-A Bay   B-E Bee   B - I - Bid-dy Bye   B   Boh Boh Bid-dy

Bye Bee Bee Bee   Bee   Bid-dy Bye   Bee   Boo Boo   Boo-boo!

1. Show a visual of the words and/or music to your singers.

2. Speak the words in rhythm. Then, have them echo you, two measures at a time.

3. Increase to four-measure echoes, and then speak the entire warm up together in rhythm.

4. Sing the song as your choir listens. Then, teach the melody by phrases.

5. When the song is learned, substitute in different consonants to replace "B" as you go up by half steps.

Hint: Consider using blended consonants, as well, such as "ch" or "fl." But beware! There are a few consonants as well as blended sounds you might want to avoid!!

....

Personal note: This is a great warm up that my students demand to do time and again.

....

SOLFEGE STACK

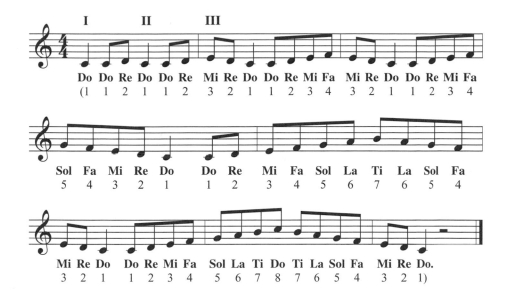

1. Sing this beginning with low "Do" or "1" and then reverse it and start with high "Do" or "8."
2. Sing it as a 2 or 3-part round.

Personal note: This is not a new idea, but it shouldn't be left out of warm up "musts."

ROW YOUR BOAT

With Sound

1. Have your choir perform the rhythm for this song on various non-voiced sounds, such as "pf," "sh," "tsk," etc.
2. Perform unison, then as a round.

AARDVARKS ARE MY FRIENDS

(to the tune of "Yankee Doodle")

Aard-varks are my friends. Aard-varks are my friends. Aard-varks are my

friends. Aard-varks are my friends. Aard-varks are my friends. Aard-varks are

my friends. Aard-varks are my friends. Aard-varks are my friends. Aard-

varks are my friends. Aard-varks are my friends. Aard-varks are my friends.

1. Write the words "Aardvarks are my friends" on a visual.

2. Explain to your students they will be substituting in these words to the familiar melody "Yankee Doodle."

3. Sing together, repeating up/down by half steps.

SOUND ROUND

To Prepare

Create a 4-measure vocalized rhythm pattern. For ex.,:

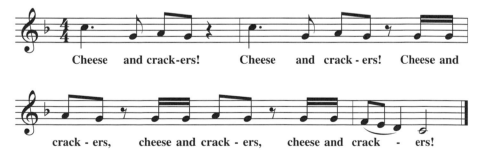

| Tsk | Tsk | Tsk | Tsk | Ch | Ch | Ch | Ch | Ch | Ch | Ch |

| Puh | Puh | Puh | Puh | Puh | Ss | Ss | Ss |

1. Teach the pattern to your singers, one measure at a time.

2. When the pattern is learned, have them perform it as a 2-, 3- or 4-part round.

3. Later, add voiced rhythms and perform the Sound Round again.

Personal note: These non-voiced sounds are great for warming up the diaphragm.

CHEESE AND CRACKERS

(to Handel's "Hallelujah Chorus")

Cheese   and crack-ers!   Cheese   and crack - ers!   Cheese and

crack - ers,   cheese and crack - ers,   cheese and crack   -   ers!

1. Sing the new words to this familiar tune, moving up/down by half steps.

2. Encourage singers to perform with "fish lips" for "cheese" and leave out the last "r" in "crack-ers" as they sing.

Personal note: Our apologies to Mr. Handel.

DADDY'S GOT A HEAD LIKE A PING PONG BALL

(to the tune of "The William Tell Overture")

1. Review the melody with your singers.

2. Add the new words.

3. Repeat, going up/down by half steps.

Personal note: This is a fun way to engage the voice! (And, our apologies to Rossini, also…)

28

TENSION BREAKERS

Use these activities during a rehearsal to help break the tension or provide a little fun for your singers after they've finished rehearsing a song. The time spent doing them is worthwhile and will help to clear the brain for the next section of rehearsal time.

EIGHT COUNT

Have singers perform the following pattern as they count aloud:

1. Reach R arm across and up overhead as you count to 8
2. Repeat with L arm in opposite direction
3. Reach R arm across and to the side as you count to 8
4. Repeat with L arm in opposite direction
5. Reach R arm across and down to L knee and count to 8
6. Repeat with L arm in opposite direction
7. Reach R arm across and down to L toe and count to 8
8. Repeat with L arm in opposite direction
9. Repeat all actions, counting to 4, then 2, then 1
10. End with a clap

Variation

This pattern also works:

Snap for 8 • Clap for 8 • Pat for 8 • Stomp for 8
Continuing using 4 counts, 2 counts, 1 count; end with a clap.

MAKING RAIN

1. Tell your students to follow the actions you demonstrate but not to begin those actions until you are facing their direction.

2. Perform the following actions, moving from the right side of your group to the left:
   - Rub hands together (a la "wind")
   - Alternately snap (a la "sprinkling")
   - Alternately pat legs (a la "rain")
   - Add stomps to pats (a la "downpour")
   - Reverse actions as the rainstorm resides

Personal note: This is not a new idea, but it's surprising how students never tire of doing it.

BOOGIE DOWN

This is a call and answer activity, which begins teacher-led and then shifts to a student-led game.

1. Have students stand and teach them this chant.

Boo - gie down,   boo - boo - gie down.   Boo - gie down,   boo -

Teacher: *Student:*   *Teacher:*   *Student:*   *Teacher:*

- boo-gie down. Hey, Car-ly! (Hey, what?) Hey, Car-ly! (Hey, what? Hey, what?) Let

Student:

___ me see you boo - gie down. Let ___ me see you boo - gie down. (With my

All:

hands in the air and my feet on the ground, this is how I boo-gie down.) With her

hands in the air and her feet on the ground, this is how she boo-gies down.

2. When "Carly" says "With my hands in the air," she responds by putting her hands in the air. Likewise, when she says "and my feet on the ground," she points to her feet. Finally, when she says, "This is how I boogie down," she does a dance (of her choice) for those 4 beats.

3. Everyone responds, "With her hands in the air and her feet on the ground, this is how she boogies down," performing the same actions "Carly" performed.

4. The game repeats, but this time "Carly" finds a student and calls them by name in the "Hey, Carly" section. "Carly" now says what the teacher said before and the new student takes the lines that belonged to "Carly."

5. The new student then becomes the next leader and the chant begins again.

Personal note: This is a great activity to use when working on learning your students' names.

LAYERING

1. Perform a 4-beat pattern and have your singers echo you. Do several of these to help establish the activity.

2. Once your singers are comfortable with this, explain that you want them to continue to echo your actions, but as they are responding, you will be performing a new action for them to echo, i.e. as a "round."

3. Perform the activity, adding background music, if desired.

Personal Note: Don't hesitate to select a student to lead this activity.

PUSH/PULL

1. To energize your group when they are looking and sounding tired, ask them to stand and push their hands to the ceiling, holding this position to the count of 10.

2. Now, ask them to push their hands to the floor without bending over and hold this position to the count of 10.

3. Finally, ask them to cup their fingers together, a la "opera position," and pull the hands in opposite direction without letting go, holding for a count of 10.

SIGHT SINGING

One of the most important things you can give your singers is the ability to sing on sight. Not only will it make learning the music much faster and understandable, but once this skill is achieved, it is something they will use for the rest of their lives. Here are some sight singing ideas to help keep your singers focused and excited about learning this challenging part of the singing process.

DRUM PATTERN

Materials

- Drums (If you don't have drums, try this simple solution. Go to the thrift store and purchase old metal pots and pans, gift boxes or anything you can bang on to get a sound. Anything can be a drum. Just use your creativity!)

To Prepare

Create a visual or handout with 8-10 measures of rhythms; number each measure.

1. Have students clap the rhythm visual.

2. Assign a group of students to each measure number. (It is best if they are sitting together with the other members of their group.)

3. Using their "drums," have them play the line of rhythm, but only their assigned measure. This helps with the ability to keep a steady beat and develops aural skills.

4. Once they have done this successfully, have them "leave out" random measures. For example, only have the odd measures play, omitting the even-numbered measures, and then vice versa.

5. Now, have the students play the line of music backwards, reading it from right to left.

Personal note: My students enjoy this more when the drums or instruments are not conventional. I have used spoons, cups, Popsicle sticks, etc. to make this more engaging.

ODDS AND EVENS

To Prepare

Create a visual or handout with 8-10 measures of sight reading music; number each measure.

1. Have the students sing the music together using solfege/numbers until somewhat learned.

2. Assign every other person to be an "odd" or an "even."

3. Ask the group to sing the line again but the odd-numbered singers will only sing the odd-numbered measures, and the even-numbered singers perform the even-numbered measures.

4. The students continue through the music, singing every other measure, depending upon whether they are an "odd" or an "even."

Personal note: Students will try to sing the entire line. Sometimes it is best to have the "evens" practice first and then the "odds" practice together. This clarifies that they are to only sing every other measure.

AROUND THE ROOM RHYTHMS

To Prepare

Write 2-3 measures of rhythm on a strip of paper (or poster board). Create several of these (different rhythms) and hang them on the wall around your room. (These can be laminated for later use.) Be sure to space them out.

1. Divide students into groups, one group per section of rhythm.

2. Have students stand in front of their rhythm hanging on the wall and practice clapping it together.

3. Ask them to rotate to the right where they will find the next rhythm. Have them practice this new pattern.

4. Continue having them move around the room until they are back at their original spot.

5. Now, explain they will be circling around the room from paper to paper to clap the rhythm papers. They will have a measure of rest in between each rhythm section in order to allow time to move.

6. Count them in to begin. Continue to move them seamlessly around the room until they are back to their original spot.

7. Do the same activity again, moving the groups in the opposite direction.

SING ON SIGHT IN ROUNDS

To Prepare

Create a visual or hand out of with 8-10 measures of sight reading music. Be sure to number the measures so that it is easy to enter as a round.

1. Have the class read the music together. Practice it several times.

2. Divide the group into two sections and have the students do the song as a round with group one starting at the beginning and group two starting one measure later.

3. Ask group one to hold the last note until group two finishes.

4. Now, divide the group into three sections. Sing in a round, having them enter in one-measure intervals.

5. Continue dividing into smaller groups until you have the same amount of groups as you do measures, singing as a round after each division.

Personal note: This is an excellent tool to use when working on part singing. It allows the members of the class to become more confident in the music as the groups get smaller.

CUP RHYTHMS

Materials

- Styrofoam cups, one for each student (Plastic cups will tear apart quickly.)

To Prepare

Create a visual or hand out of with 4-6 measures of rhythms

1. Hand out the cups and teach the following rhythm responses for each note value they will be reading: (Begin with cups upside down in laps)

   - **Quarter note (ta)** = tap cup in lap

   - **Half note (ta-a)** = tap cup lap for 1st beat; slide forward for 2nd

   - **Dotted half note (ta-a-a)** = tap cup in lap for 1st beat, slide forward for 2nd and slide back for 3rd

   - **Whole note (ta-a-a-a)** = tap cup in lap for 1st beat, slide forward for 2nd, slide back for 3rd and slide forward for 4th

   - **Two Eighth notes (ti-ti)** = tap cup bottom with the palm of your other hand two times

2. Demonstrate how to perform the first measure of rhythm using a cup. Then, have students do the first measure with their cups.

3. Continue demonstrating measure by measure until the end of the song. After each measure, have the students repeat the process.

4. Practice performing the entire rhythm as a class with the cups.

5. Now, have one half of the group do the rhythm as written while the other half performs the line backwards.

....

Personal note: This is one of my students' absolute favorite ways to study rhythm. When they come in and see the cup under their chairs, they get excited for what will happen next.

....

38

CLAIM A NAME

To Prepare
Create a visual or handout with 8-10 measures of sight reading music

1. Assign each student a solfege name or number. For example, the first student would be "Do/1," the next would be "Re/2," etc.

2. Ask the singers to read the music together, but have the students raise their hand every time their solfege/number name is sung.

3. Sing the line a second time, but have the students only sing on their solfege/number name.

4. Continue doing this until the group is secure with their part. Then, reassign names and do again.

Advanced Additional Steps

1. Once singers are secure with the music, begin removing "names." (It is best *not* to remove Do/1, Mi/3 and Sol/5 until the last attempts.)

2. Tell students, "Sing the music again, but if you are Re/2, don't sing."

3. Continue taking away students' solfege names until all that is left is Do/1. When you are at this step, begin adding the names back in, one at a time.

Enhancement Idea
Use boom whackers or tone chimes when reading the music.

MEET IN THE MIDDLE

To Prepare

Create a visual or handout with 8-10 measures of sight reading music

1. Have students sing a line of music from the beginning to the end.
2. Now, ask them to sing it from the end to the beginning.
   (Yes, do it backwards!)
3. Have the singers count the notes and find the middle note/pitch and circle it on their paper (or mark it on the visual) so that it stands out.
4. Divide the class in half and have one group start in the beginning and the other at the end of the piece.
5. When they reach the note in the very center of the piece, have them hold it and perform a crescendo and decrescendo.
6. On your cue, have them continue on in the same direction they began.

Enhancement Opportunity

Do this activity as described, but when they reach the middle note, have them travel in the opposite direction from where they started. For example, the first group would start at the beginning, hit the middle note and then go backward to the beginning with the second group doing the opposite.

Personal note: This is an excellent way to begin singers reading in parts. It is fun and challenging, making it seem less like a chore and more like a game.

TRASHKETBALL

Materials

- Basketball
- Round trash can (or something that can receive a tossed basketball)

To Prepare

Several 4-beat solfege flashcards incorporating many pitches and rhythm patterns.

1. Divide your singers into small groups (4-5 people).

2. Show the first group one of the solfege cards.

3. This group has 10 seconds to look at the card. After that time, they must sight read the card using solfege/numbers and hand signs.

4. If, as a group, they read the card correctly, one of the team members is given the opportunity to shoot the basketball into the can. If the "basket scores," that team receives a point.

....

Personal note: This is another idea I wish we knew who to credit. It also can be adapted to any sport. For football, create a small football field visual with footballs representing various teams. These can advance by 5 yards with correct answers. For baseball, each correct response will be rewarded with a hit, etc.

....

FIVE TO STAY ALIVE

Because five minutes is generally the amount of time spent in a sight reading room at contest, this activity involves five minutes of concentrated time directed at singing on sight.

Materials

- Timer

To Prepare

Gather various sight reading exercises. Some of these need to be unpitched rhythms-only; others need to be pitched exercises. They can be original or pulled from some of the previous ideas listed in this book.

Procedure

Minute 1: Rhythm Reading

These rhythms can be of various lengths. It will be whatever you need to fill the five minutes allotted for this part of the activity. Consider using these activities as mentioned in this book: "Cup Rhythms," "Drum Pattern," "Body Created Rhythm," or simply clap a rhythm written on a visual.

Minutes 2 and 3: Repeat It, Sign It, Sing It

See the instructions for this activity on page 48.

Minutes 4 and 5: Sight Singing

Again, this music can be of your choosing. Consider using some of the ideas found in this book:

- Meet in the Middle (page 40)
- Sing on Sight in Rounds (page 37)
- Odds and Evens (page 35)
- Claim a Name (page 39)

or any other resource of your choosing, as long as it fills the minutes needed.

1. Select a student to be your timer for this activity. (I have the same timer for the entire week.)

2. Make the students aware of the procedure. Once established, it will become a daily habit and will not need to be reviewed.

Personal note: It is my belief that a choir can learn to sight read proficiently when practicing this skill five minutes a day. On a normal week, this means that your choir is sight reading for 45 minutes. Nine weeks of this practice means your choir has studied for a total of 225 minutes. If you can find a way to incorporate aural skills, kinesthetic learning, and fun into the five minutes, they will look forward to the study time. I have seen this happen year after year. Five to Stay Alive is the format I use daily in my classroom. The students know what to expect, while still not being sure exactly how it will all play out. There is also an element of fun, which keeps them engaged at all times.

MAGIC RHYTHM SQUARES

To Prepare

Draw eight squares (four on the top row and four directly underneath) on a board or visual. In each square, write a 4-beat rhythm. These can either be random rhythms or the eight measures could be taken from a phrase in a song you are working on or getting ready to teach. (These rhythms need to be something you can erase, remove or cover up.)

1. Review the rhythm of each square found on the board as you clap and rhythm speak. (Spend time having them recognize "like rhythms" if this is an option.)

2. Work through the squares one row at a time and collectively. Practice until the students are somewhat secure with the rhythms as a whole.

3. Have the class close their eyes as you remove (erase/cover) one of the squares.

4. Ask them to open their eyes and clap all of the squares again, even the missing one.

5. Continue this process, one square at a time, until all squares are missing.

6. Now, ask them to write in each square until it reappears.

Personal note: If using this idea to teach a section of a song, after the activity, see if students can find where these eight measures are found in the music. This is great fun!

HALL OF FAME

Materials

- Simple prizes that can be used as "awards," i.e. medals to wear around the necks at concerts, pins, ribbons, paper certificates, concert program recognitions, (or a combination thereof)
- Hall of Fame poster board to autograph

To Prepare

Create or find 5-10 sight-reading lines that are consistent with the ability level of your students. Put these on a handout (or display on a visual).

Rules for getting into the "Hall of Fame"

- Students get one chance at sight singing a line of music.
- Any error means you must stop, but you can try again on another Hall of Fame Ceremony Day.
- Only 5–10 members of the choir can try sight singing on a Ceremony Day.
- Singers must sing and sign accurately, in order to earn their way into the Hall of Fame.
- Singers must perform alone.

(Continued on the next page.)

45

Procedure

1. Have the students stand who would like to try out for the Hall of Fame.

2. Begin with the first student and have him/her sing the first line of music.

3. The next student sings the second line, etc. (Please note: If you do not use a fresh line of sight reading material for each student, it is not fair to the group. It must be new to each singer.)

4. Continue until all of those interested have had an opportunity to sing.

5. When done, the ones who were accurate in their reading can sign the Hall of Fame poster board and become a Hall of Fame member.

Personal note: I do a Hall of Fame Ceremony Day once a month. Interestingly, I have found the most important recognition in the eyes of my students is getting to sign their autograph on the "Hall of Fame" poster board for that school year. It is then laminated and remains hung on the wall for all to see. Students from nine or ten years ago will come back to visit and immediately point out their name on the Hall of Fame posters. It is also important to recognize the efforts of those that did not read accurately. I keep a chart and place a sticker by their name. If they tryout four times and don't get in, the four stickers allow them to "make an error" the next time they try out and it not be held against them. I have had students try out all semester and finally make the Hall of Fame because they have enough "stickers" to carry them through. I am always most proud of those students, because it didn't come easy for them yet they kept trying.

EAR TRAINING

Just as sight singing is to the eyes, ear training is to the ears. Before we can ever read words, we must hear them…over and over. Ear training permits singers to hear pitches and intervals, allowing them to vocalize and later read. Don't underestimate the positive results from spending time doing this on a regular basis.

REPEAT IT, SIGN IT, SING IT

To Prepare

Decide what intervals and solfege syllables you want your students to learn for this lesson

Step 1: Repeat It

1. Sing a simple melodic pattern while using the hand signs for solfege. For example, "Do Mi Mi," "Do Do Do," "Do Re Mi," etc.

2. Students should mimic your actions.

3. Repeat this several times with different pitches. (We usually do 8.)

Step 2: Sign It

1. Sing the melodic intervals of step one, but do not use the coordinating hand signs.

2. Students process what the teacher sang and, in turn, *only* do the hand signs. (The students **do not** sing in this step. They only sign.)

Step 3: Sing It

1. Now, *sign* the melodic intervals for the class, but do not sing them.

2. Students process what they saw and then sing back the intervals without signing.

Enhancement Idea

The teacher can actually sing the syllables (Do, Re, Mi,) or sing on "loo," depending on the ability level of the group. The latter is more difficult to accomplish.

....

Personal note: This is an excellent activity when you are beginning to teach sight singing. It teaches students to recognize pitch in its relation to the hand symbols for solfege, develop strong listening skills, work on tuning/matching pitch, and allow the teacher the opportunity to assess the learned skills. We do this every day in my choir classroom, and found this to be a perfect time to have a student aide take attendance, hand out papers, etc. This helps to streamline the beginning of the class period. It also establishes that solfege skills will be worked every day.

....

CHROMATIC TUNING

1. Divide students into three sections and have each section sit together. (Consider using "altos," "sopranos" and "men," if this would work.)

2. Ask all students to sing the same pitch ("Do" or "number," depending on your note reading system.)

3. Point up or down to one of the sections. That section moves vocally one step in the direction you have pointed. Sing on "loo" or, for a more advanced approach, have them continue to use solfege/numbers.

4. Keep moving that section or point to and move another section.

5. Continue this process, moving the sections up, down, etc., until you end up with a tuned chord, i.e. I, IV, and V chords work nicely.

....

Personal Note: The easiest thing to do is to move them to a I chord, then adjust into a IV chord, then a simple movement here and there to a V chord, settling back to a I chord.

....

THINK THE TRIAD

1. Have your singers review a major triad by singing and signing these pitches.

2. Once familiar, ask them to sing up and down the scale using solfege/numbers, but to audiate the triad, keeping those pitches silent.

3. Reverse this idea, only singing the triad pitches while audiating the others.

4. Review a different triad and practice again.

MUSICAL SIMON FOR TWO

1. Have your singers find a partner.
2. The first student sings a pitch.
3. The second student must sing that pitch and add his/her own pitch.
4. The first student then repeats the pitches given in the order they were presented, adding his/her own at the end.
5. Play continues until one of the singers misses singing the pitch sequence.

MUSICAL SIMON FOR FOUR

1. Have four students sit in chairs that have been placed in a small circle.
2. Ask each to sing a pitch of their choice. (Each pitch must be different.)
3. Select two "players" from your class.
4. Player 1 taps the head of one of the singers. That person sings his/her pitch.
5. Player 2 then taps the head of the first singer and then chooses another pitch/singer (or it could be the same pitch/singer).
6. Players continue back and forth until one misses the sequence of pitches.

LISTENING BEE

1. Review intervals with your singers and what each one sounds like. (For beginners, stick with the major intervals and work with the minor ones after they are successful with these.)

2. For a better understanding and to help them remember these sounds, associate a song that uses these same intervals. For example,

   2nd = "Happy Birthday"

   3rd = "Oh, When the Saints"

   4th = "Here Comes the Bride"

   5th = "Twinkle, Twinkle Little Star"

   6th = "My Bonnie Lies Over the Ocean"

   7th = "Bali Hai" (or, as my students call this interval, it sounds like something from "Psycho")

   8th (or octave) = "Somewhere Over the Rainbow"

3. After the review, challenge each student to listen to an interval and name it correctly. (Winners could win a monetary prize like a piece of candy or sticker.)

Variation

Play a game by dividing your group into teams. Play an interval for Team 1. The first person in that group has to name the interval. If correct, their team gets a point. If incorrect, the first person on Team 2 has the opportunity to steal the point by naming the interval correctly. Play continues back and forth until all players have had an opportunity to name a pitch.

Personal note: This is a non-threatening activity/game that sometimes highlights my students who might not be the best vocalists, but have a wonderful "ear."

BACK-TO-BACK

1. Choose a round familiar to your students and have them practice singing it in unison.

2. Have your students find a partner and practice singing this song as a round with their partner while standing back-to-back.

3. Repeat this process, having singers turn and stand face-to-face.

Personal note: This idea builds great singing independence and also makes your singers listen to each other better than if they sing the round in a group.

SILENT SINGING

1. Select a song to sing (or one of the choral pieces you are working on).

2. Explain you are going to have them sing aloud as well as silently throughout the song.

3. Show them the signals you will use for each, for example, "thumbs up" for aloud and "thumbs down" for silently.

4. Have your students sing as you direct, indicating sound on/off throughout.

GAMES

Most students thrive off of this part of the learning process. They end up having so much fun, they don't realize how much they've learned. Consequently, they ask to repeat these activities again and again, which is a win-win for the student and teacher. These games included can begin a rehearsal, break up rehearsal time or be the entire class lesson.

ONE AND TWO

1. Number the students "one" or "two."

2. Have students stand and look at your hands. Explain that your right hand is number "one" and your left hand, number "two."

3. Explain that all of the "ones" should follow with their bodies what your right hand does, and the "twos" should follow your left hand.

4. Lean your *right* hand to the left and right, bend it, etc. Students should bend their bodies to follow your hand.

5. Repeat the same actions with your *left* hand as the "two's" respond.

6. Now, move both hands together with the same actions as each group follows the assigned hand.

7. After the students get used to the movements, have the hands do different things.

8. At this point in the activity, when a student misses a cue or does it incorrectly, he/she sits down.

9. Play until you have a winner(s).

Personal note: This is an excellent activity to begin the year. It emphasizes the need to watch the director. It is also a great way to stretch.

FOCUS

1. Begin by explaining to your singers what you expect to see from them in reference to performance behavior, i.e. hands to side, eyes on director, etc.

2. Divide your choir into teams. This can either be "left side/right side," "sopranos-tenors/altos-basses" or whatever division that provides close to equal numbers in each section.

3. Select a performance song to sing.

4. Say "5 – 4 – 3 – 2 – 1 – Focus." From then on until the end of the song, all singers stay focused, following performance etiquette. If you should catch anyone not following this procedure, point at them and say, "Caught ya." That singer must then either put a finger in the air or be seated (your choice.)

5. At the end of the song, count the number of singers caught. The team with the least number wins the game.

THINKING AHEAD WITH "ROW YOUR BOAT"

1. Sing the song "Row Your Boat." Each time you sing, leave off a word until the song finally "disappears."

2. If a student sings past the last word, he/she is out and must be seated.

Personal note: This is another idea to help your singers understand the importance of thinking ahead.

SING THE ALPHABET

1. Challenge your students to sing the alphabet on a 5-tone descending/ascending pattern, i.e. "sol-fa-mi-re-do-re-mi-fa-sol," etc. in one breath.

2. As they run out of air, they should be seated. See which singers are able to make it to the end. Those who make it through the alphabet are the winners.

3. Repeat the process, encouraging those who sat to see if they can get further in the alphabet than before.

Personal note: This one is great for developing proper air control for singing long phrases.

LASER TAG

1. Tell your singers they are going to play laser tag and their pointer fingers are the guns.

2. Point to a student. The two singers sitting to the right and left of this student stand and sing (on any pitch), "Beep, beep, beep," etc. while pointing their "laser guns" at each other.

3. The singer who runs out of air first loses the game.

Personal note: This is a wonderful game for developing breath control. Your men's chorus will especially like this one.

STING RHYTHM

1. Explain to your singers they will be echoing 4-beat rhythm patterns that you clap. They should echo clap *all* of the rhythms, except the "sting" rhythm (which you designate.) If they do, they are out of the game. Tell them also that if they do *not* clap a rhythm back they think is the "sting" one (and it is not), they are also out.

2. Clap the "sting" rhythm for the students several times so that they can hear what it sounds like.

3. Play the game as you clap the rhythms and they respond. Those who echo back the sting rhythm or do not clap when they should, sit down.

4. Play until you have a winner(s).

Variation: STING MELODY

This is the same idea as Sting Rhythm except that melodic patterns are used instead.

....

Personal note: This reverse idea to "Simon Says" is one of the best games ever. As students love to play this game over and over. They don't realize how great it is for training the ear.

....

57

NOTE DETECTIVE

1. Using solfege/numbers, clap or sing a phrase from a song on which you've been working.

2. See which student can be the first to name the song or find where this phrase is found in the song.

SOLFEGE SPELLING BEE

To Prepare

Create 4-beat melodic flashcards.

1. Form a line with your students.

2. Display a flashcard to the first person in the line. He/she must sing the card using solfege. If correct, he/she stays in the line. With a miss, he/she is eliminated from the game.

3. Continue the game until a winner is named.

Variation: RHYTHM SPELLING BEE

Players perform 4-beat rhythms instead of melodies.

ONE MEASURE AT A TIME

1. Select a song you have been working on.
2. Tell your choir to sing a measure and then "think" a measure.
3. Those who sing when they shouldn't are out of the game.

ONE WORD AT A TIME

1. Select a song you have been working on.
2. Find a part of the song where all singers sing the same line/melody.
3. Go down the row, having students recite by memory the lyrics to this section, one word at a time.
4. If a singer misses a word, he/she is out.
5. If the music allows, have the students *sing* these lyrics as they recite them.

Variation

Divide into two teams and shift the lyrics back and forth. The team with the most students left standing at the end of the lyric section, wins the game.

Personal note: This is a great game when trying to memorize lyrics or for checking to see if they are learned.

POM

1. Select a song you have been working on.
2. Tell your singers they will only sing the first beat of each measure and audiate the remaining notes.
3. Any student who sings when he/she should not, is out of the game.

Personal note: This game helps improve audiation skills.

DON'T BREAK THE EGG!

1. Select a song you have been working on.

2. Tell your singers they will be humming this song instead of singing it.

3. Explain you want them to imagine they are putting a raw egg (that's in the shell) in their mouth to create the space for the hum.

4. As they sing, if you see someone whose mouth is not in the correct shape to hold the egg, point to them and say, "Your egg is cracked." They are then eliminated from the game.

Personal note: This one is super for creating space in the mouth.

SOLFEGE STACK–THE GAME

1. Follow the procedures for learning the Solfege Stack vocalise found on page 25.

2. Once reviewed, ask your singers to audiate or leave out one of the solfege/numbers in the vocalise, for example, "mi/3."

3. If they sing this pitch aloud as they are performing the vocalise, they are out.

4. Play a second round leaving out an additional solfege pitch or number, for example, "sol/5." Those who sing either "mi/3" or "sol/5" are eliminated from the game.

Variation

Without playing this as a game, use this as a vocalise, leaving out the solfege/numbers of your choice. Also, perform this as a round with the missing solfege/numbers.

MUSICAL DARTS

Materials

- Dartboard (which you will hang)
- Several plastic darts (Extra plastic darts are a great idea, as they tend to break at times.)

To Prepare

1. Make a set of flash cards consisting of 10 cards each for the number of teams you will have. Place on the cards musical terms, pitches or rhythms you want your class to learn. The sets should be completely different with no identical cards. Draw on the floor a "throw line" where students will begin play.

2. Divide the class into teams. (Three teams are ideal, but this will depend upon your class size.) Give each team a set of flashcards and tell them they have five minutes to learn all of the cards. Explain that if they really want to win the game, all team members should know them well. At the end of five minutes, rotate the card sets and time them again to learn the new set. Continue this process until all sets have been reviewed. Explain the game rules and play the game.

Game Rules

1. One person from each team comes forward to throw a dart at the dartboard. The player whose dart hits the highest point value stays, and the others return to their teams.

2. The teacher shows a flashcard (selected from any stack) to the winning student who then recalls the answer to the card. For example, if the card is a music term, the student must give the definition. If it is a rhythm, he/she must clap it correctly using rhythm counting. If it is a pitch, he/she must give the correct solfege name for the key in which it is found.

3. If the student responds correctly, his/her team gets the value of the dart throw. If the student is unsure of the answer, he/she may ask the team, but will receive half of the value of the dart throw.

4. Continue until all students have had a chance to throw the dart.

PAPER PLATE MEMORY

To Prepare

Using inexpensive paper plates, draw a music symbol on one plate and the name of the symbol on a different plate. Do several of these. Here are some examples of symbols you might use:

Crescendo

Decrescendo

Sforzando   *sfz*

Quarter Note

Half Note

Whole Note

Quarter Rest

1. Hand out the paper plates to several of your students. This group will be the holders for the game, but will not participate in playing. Have them sit on the ground and hold the plates on the top of their heads with the drawn part not showing to the players.

2. The first player selects two students to turn over their cards. If the cards match (meaning one card shows a symbol and the other the definition), that player collects the cards and the next student has a turn. If the two cards do *not* match, the holders turn the cards back over and play continues for the next player.

3. The player with the most matches at the end of the game wins.

4. Scramble locations of the cards and play again.

Personal note: Students enjoy making the plates themselves. By allowing them to create the game, they are more apt to remember the information given.

SNAP CLAP PAT STOMP

To Prepare

Practice beforehand saying several series of physical commands in order to move quickly with the class.

1. Have students stand.
2. Using a steady beat say, "clap clap clap clap." Students physically echo the given instructions.
3. Repeat this process for "stomp stomp stomp stomp," "pat pat pat pat" and "snap snap snap snap."
4. Now that students understand each movement, mix them up. For example,
   - "snap clap clap pat"
   - "pat pat stomp pat"
   - "clap stomp pat stomp" (difficult)
   - "stomp pat clap snap" (difficult)
5. Students sit when they don't respond correctly. Play until you have a "winner."

MUSICAL CHARADES

To Prepare:

As a review, make flash cards (keep them simple) with terms you have taught in class. Here are some examples, but feel free to fine tune to your specific needs.

Crescendo	Sforzando	Staccato	Slur
Decrescendo	Dolce	Accent	Tie

1. Divide class into even teams.
2. Teams take turn sending one person to "act out" the term.
3. The person is handed a card with a word on it and then acts it out for his/her team.
4. If the team guesses correctly, they get a point. If they guess incorrectly, the card moves to the next team.

Personal note: This is a great deal of FUN! Consider using holiday songs or popular songs from the radio on other occasions.

MUSICAL SIMON SAYS

To Prepare

Think of a name for yourself that easily rolls off the tongue, something like "Miss M says" or " Mr. B says."

1. Have students stand. Explain they will be playing the game Simon Says in "Miss M style."

2. Say, "Miss M says clap twice." Students respond.

3. Continue with other activities, moving quickly.

4. Every now and then, ask them to do an action where you DON'T say "Miss M says." Students that do the activity are out and sit down.

5. Once students get used to the game, include musical concepts.

Musical Concepts to Add

- Miss M says clap a ta (clap a quarter note)

- Miss M says clap ti-ti (eighth notes)

- Miss M says clap ta-ah (half note)

- Miss M says clap a dotted half note

- Miss M says clap a whole note

- Miss M says sing a "Do" (or any other method of sight singing)

- Miss M says sing a "Re" (and so on up the scale)

Other Movement Type Items to Consider

- hop once
- hop twice
- clap twice (snap, stomp, pat, etc.)
- lean right
- lean left
- face the back of the room
- raise your arms
- put arms down
- wave hands
- close your eyes
- stand on one foot

TEACHING THE SONG

There are many ways to introduce a song to singers. To help add variety to this process, here are some ideas you may or may not have used, but can assist in keeping your singers engaged.

HUNT THE WORD

1. Play the melody you want your singers to learn on the piano (or sing on "loo") as they follow along in their music.

2. Randomly stop and ask the students on which word you stopped.

3. Start at the beginning of the phrase and play again, stopping at various places throughout.

4. Work your way through the song, beginning the game at different spots in the music.

MEMORIZATION PLATES

To Prepare

On inexpensive paper plates, write the words to a familiar song (or one line from music you are working on), one word per plate.

1. Sing through the song you will be using.

2. Hand several students a paper plate with the lyrics.

3. Time these students on how long it takes them to put the song words in order by having them stand in a row, side by side. Check for accuracy.

4. Ask the other students to sing the song while looking at the plates.

5. Point to one of the plate holders and have him/her to turn his/her plate around so it cannot be read.

6. Sing the song again, but omit the word that has been turned around.

7. Continue pointing to students to turn their plates around. Each time you omit a plate, have the class sing without the omitted words.

8. Eventually you will be left with one or two words.

Personal note: This is a very helpful tool when memorizing foreign language selections.

ONE PHRASE AT A TIME

1. Play four phrases of a song you are learning on a piano (or sing on "loo").

2. As you sing, hold up fingers to denote which phrase you are presenting. Do this several times.

3. When the singers are familiar with the phrases, randomly select one phrase to play (or sing on "loo").

4. Challenge them to figure out which one was performed.

SOLFEGE IS ALWAYS GOOD

1. Find a place in the song that can be sung with solfege, avoiding chromatic passages (unless your singers are proficient using altered pitches).

2. If the music is written in three parts, begin by having all singers read each line together with solfege/numbers and hand signs.

3. Later, divide your singers into two groups and solfege/number read two of the three parts.

4. Add the 3rd part once the two parts are achieved, and rotate the lines between the groups so that all singers experience each one.

5. Finally, assign the melodic lines to the correct vocal group.

Personal note: When my students first learn the music through solfege, they sing in tune and remember their pitches much better!

DRAW THE MELODY

Material

- Pencil and paper for each student

1. Ask singers to listen as you play (or sing on "loo") one of the melodic phrases found in a song you are learning.

2. Explain they will listen again, but this time they are to close their eyes and imagine what the melody would look like if the noteheads were connected with a line.

3. After you have finished singing this the second time, ask them to draw on their papers what the melodic line looked like to them.

4. Now, have them hunt through the music (or the section you are introducing) to see if they can find a melodic phrase in the music that resembles their drawing.

5. Once discovered, have them sing the melody together on "loo" (or solfege/numbers, if capable).

6. If this melodic line is found in any other section or part of the song, see if they can discover where it is.

7. Continue this process for as many lines as you would like to reinforce or learn.

TRICKS FOR BETTER SINGING

We don't claim to be masters of this area, but we owe so much to many of our peers and predecessors for their knowledge shared. If you've not tried these ideas listed, give them a go and see if they help to make your choir sound better!

RIBBON SING

Vocal problems addressed

- Breathing too frequently
- Unable to sing through long musical phrases

Materials

- A yard of ribbon, string or yarn, one for each student (strips of fabric work, as well)

1. Ask students to sing a phrase of music they are having a difficult time performing in one breath.

2. Now, have them take the ribbon and slowly pull it through one hand with the other.

3. Have them breath in deeply and perform this action again, but this time to slowly exhale while the ribbon is moving.

4. Ask how many were able to keep the air moving and not run out of breath.

5. Sing the line of music again as students pull the ribbon through their hands. (You will find the more you do this, the more they will be able to achieve the extended breathing needed to make the phrase musical.)

RAINBOW DYNAMICS

Vocal problems addressed

- A lack of musicality in a line of music

- Music that has height in the middle of the line but unsupported with breath

- Problems with phrasing and creating dynamics

1. Ask students to sing a phrase of music that is challenging them dynamically.

2. Now, have them place their right hand on top of their left, palms touching.

3. Ask them to create a rainbow with their right hand.

4. Discuss the dynamics you need in the phrase of music previously sung.

5. Explain they are going to start singing this line with a sensitive volume and as their "rainbow" gains height, they will increase their volume. They will also need to decrease and have a more sensitive volume when the rainbow arches back down.

6. Have students sing the line of music while creating a rainbow with their hands and voices.

Personal note: When I conduct my choirs in a concert and practice, I actually make the rainbow while I am conducting. This reminds them of the phrasing of the piece and is a quick visual aid to keep them on track.

TURN UP THE RADIO, PLEASE

Vocal problem addressed

* Lack of appropriate dynamics

1. Have students count from 1 to 8 aloud and then back down from 8 to 1.

2. Discuss the numbers found on a stereo knob.

3. Tell your singers they are going to sing on "ah," but they need to start at volume one from the radio dial, increase their volume up to eight and then decrease back down to one.

4. Have them put their hands out as if to turn a stereo volume knob.

5. With your students following you, turn the knob to different volumes as they sing "ah." (You will need to say the numbers aloud for them.)

6. Have students sing a phrase of music while watching you turn their volume up and down, using your imaginary stereo knob.

Personal note: Don't hesitate to actually turn the knob during rehearsal or concert. Students respond to what they do in class when there is a visual aid to tie it all together.

UNHINGE IT

Vocal problems addressed

- Lack of a dropped jaw
- Lack of an open tone

1. Have students sing an "ah" vowel together on the same pitch.

2. Ask them to place two fingers in front of their ears and have them open their mouths wide.

3. Point out that the jaw hinge can be felt when they open their mouth.

4. Have students sing the "ah" vowel again but with their fingers checking for the unhinged jaw.

5. Now, ask them to sing "ah, eh, ee, oh, oo" with their jaw unhinged.

6. Call attention to the fact that the "ee" vowel is the only vowel in which the hinge closes.

7. Have the students sing a line of music while "checking the hinge."

Personal note: When I tell my choirs to "drop their jaw," I get a varying amount from everyone. I have found that when I tell them to "unhinge," the look and sound is more uniform from all the singers involved.

COLOR IT/AGE IT

Vocal problems addressed

- Shallow vowels
- Too bright of tone
- Lack of depth and richness in the sound

Color It

1. If, after students sing, you hear too bright of a tone, tell them their sound was a nice "hot pink" or "bright yellow."

2. Now, ask them to sing the line again in a " deep brown" or "dark blue" color. *(This will shift the tone to a richer, more mature sound.)*

3. Continue naming colors, having them sing until you hear the tone you are looking for. Below is a list of colors you might consider using:

   - Hot Pink
   - Purple
   - Bright Yellow
   - Dark Blue
   - Sky Blue
   - Deep Brown
   - Grassy Green

Age It

This is just like "Color It," but with labels sound with different ages.

1. Ask students to sing a line of music so you can decide how old they are.

2. If they sound like they are "10 years old," ask them to sing like they are 15 instead.

3. Continue giving ages until you hear the desired tone.

STOP THE SOUND

Vocal problem addressed

- "Oo" vowel

1. Ask students to sing an "oo" vowel.
2. Have them check to see if they have the correct mouth shape by placing their index finger into their mouth opening. If their finger stops the sound, they have the correct shape needed.

SING A "G"

1. Ask students to sing a "G" (above middle C) on command. On the first try, unless you have a singer with perfect pitch, most will be close, but not many will know exactly where the note is.
2. Give the choir the note from a keyboard. Have them match the pitch and ask them to close their eyes and think about where this pitch lies in their throat/head.
3. Do this several times in a rehearsal and continue to do this on a daily/ weekly basis. You will be amazed at how good your singers (and you) will get at finding this pitch the first time!

Personal note: This is a wonderful way to help your choir develop relative pitch. Believe it or not, it really does work!

OPEN MOUTH "S" / CONNECT THE "S"

Vocal problems addressed

- "S" consonant when cutting off (hanging over the hiss)
- "S" consonant found in a held word (making a hissing sound within a phrase)

Open Mouth "S"

1. Have the students hiss an "S" sound for a long period of time.

2. Ask them to try to cut off the "S" at the same time. (This will most likely not work and some students' sound will hang over.)

3. Have singers try to make an "S" sound (hiss) with their mouths open.

4. Point out it is not possible to do this with the mouth in this position.

5. Have them hiss an "S" sound, but on your cue, open their mouths a bit.

6. Continue doing this exercise until they can all stop at the same time.

7. Now, sing the word "has" (or another "s" ending word of your choice), holding it for a while and then end the "S" with an open mouth.

8. Continue doing this until the end is clear.

Connect the "S"

1. Find a phrase in your music that has a held word with an "S" ending. For example:

2. In this example, both the words "sometimes" and "motherless" have held notes with an "S" ending. Tell students to hold the vowel in the phrase until the last possible moment; then change to the next word by placing the "S." Therefore, "Some-times I feel" would be "Some-time sl feel." "Mo-ther-less child" would be "mo-ther-le-sschild." This cleans up a carried over "S."

ACTION ASSOCIATION

Vocal problem addressed

• Performing articulations, phrasing or lyrics in the music

1. Ask your singers to perform a kinesthetic motion with you as they sing the word or phrase in the song desiring a certain musical element, i.e. staccato, legato, tenuto, etc. For example, to help perform a "staccato" in the music, first have your students practice placing their right index finger into the palm of their left hand and touch it quickly as if the palm is a hot iron.

2. Ask them to sing a vocalise using a staccato. As they sing, have them perform the kinesthetic motion described above.

3. Now, reference this element in your music and have them practice the action together while singing this part of the song.

4. Later, when directing the group, perform the motion for the singers during the section of music that requires the staccato.

Other actions to consider

• Punch the air for an accent

• Kneed some bread by pushing the palms of your hands together for tenuto

• Paint in the air for legato

• For lyrics, assign an action for that word during rehearsal. Then, when the word occurs in the performance, you can add that motion into your directing to help singers remember the word.

77

LIPS, LIPS, LIPS

Vocal problem addressed

- The "ee," "oh" and "oo" vowels

1. Have your students sing an "ee," "oh" or "oo" vowel.
2. If you see they are spreading the vowel and need more of a "fish lip" shape, have them place their index finger from their nose to their chin.
3. While singing, if their lips touch their finger similar to the feel they get from saying "shhhh," they have the correct shape needed for these vowels sounds.

Hint: For singers to check and see if they have good "fish lips," have them make a circle with their index finger connected to their thumb, similar to the sign they use for "Ok." Ask them to place their lips in their fingers. This will help to create the "fish lips" needed.

PAPER STACK

Vocal problem addressed

- Tuning on repeated pitches

1. Select a pitch and ask your singers to sing it over and over.
2. As they sing the first pitch, have them hold out one of their hands, palm down.
3. On the second pitch, ask them to place the palm of the other hand on top of the back of the first hand.
4. One the third pitch, the bottom hand comes out from underneath and is placed on top of the second hand and so on, as if stacking papers on top of each other. This will have an amazing effect on keeping the pitches in tune.
5. Then, apply this idea to the music you are singing.

Personal note: There is something that happens with the lift of the hands that guides the voice to follow.

78

RUBBER BANDS

Vocal problem addressed

- Phrasing

Materials

- One rubber band for each student

1. Find a phrase in your music that needs more dynamic or tension contrast.
2. Ask students to take the rubber bands and create tension as they sing toward the middle of the phrase and then release the tension at the end of the phrase.
3. Relate the tension to the muscles in their diaphragm that help with phrasing changes.

TENNIS BALL MOUTH

Vocal problem addressed

- Dropping the jaw

To Prepare

Take a tennis ball and cut a mouth opening on the seam.
(For fun, add eyes to help them envision a face. You can even give it a name!)

1. Ask students to sing a section of music.
2. If you notice their mouths are not open enough, pull up the tennis ball and pinch the sides together that are next to the slit opening. The mouth of the tennis ball drops beautifully to create the shape you need from your singers. Surprisingly, they mimic this shape!

79

LIP BUZZING

Vocal problem addressed

- Lack of breath support

1. Have students sing from "sol/5" down to "do/1" while buzzing their lips.
2. Now, repeat the action from "do/1" up to "sol/5."
3. Create other melodic patterns for them to "buzz."

Personal note: There is no way for them be able to do this correctly without the use of a deep breath and pushing from the diaphragm. If they are unable to do this exercise, tongue trills work as well.

UNICORN HORNS

Vocal problem addressed

- Focused sound (especially for high pitches)

1. If you hear your singers spreading the sound too much while singing, ask them to pretend they are unicorns and the sound is coming out of their horn in the middle of their head.
2. As they sing, have them try to spear the sound with their horns. There are usually some giggles with this request, but it helps the sound tremendously!

FIX THE TEACHER

Vocal problem addressed

- Understanding choral technique needed for good singing

1. Demonstrate a passage in a section of music by singing poorly, using bad diction, vowel shape, support or a combination of all.
2. After singing, ask a student(s) to "fix" you by telling you what you need to do in order to achieve a better sound.

Personal note: They will be amazed (and you will, too) at what they don't realize they know!

END WITH AN "UH"

Vocal problem addressed

- Ending consonant sound

1. In order to create a more defined ending to a word, especially one found at the end of a phrase (for example, "find"), ask your singer to perform in the way they have been singing and to listen for the ending consonant.
2. Discuss whether it was good or bad sound.
3. Now, have them sing this phrase again, but this time ask them to put a small "uh" at the end of the word. For example, "find" would sound like this: "find-uh." The lift used on the end will help place the consonant together and make the letter "sparkle."

TAKE THE "R" OUT

Vocal problem addressed

- Closing the vowel to the "r" sound

1. If you find that your choir is closing words that contain "r's" in them, for example, "father," "mercy," etc., simply ask them to sing the words without the "r."

2. To help demonstrate the difference, ask them to over emphasize the "r" while speaking/singing these words.

3. Now, have them speak/sing the same words without the "r." The vowel opens and the sound becomes pure and unified.

Personal note: There are times when you don't want to dismiss the "r" entirely. This would be a stylistic choice and should be used at your discretion.

MUSIC WRITING AND THEORY FUN

Here are some ways to reinforce what you're already teaching in class on a daily basis. These ideas will offer your singers another creative outlet for expressing music.

BODY-CREATED RHYTHM

To Prepare

Write 4-6 simple 4-beat rhythms on a board or visual. It is best to use non-syncopated or complex rhythms.

1. Have students clap rhythms found on the visual to ensure understanding.

2. Show the class how to use body percussion for the first rhythm. For example, "ta ta ta ta" could be four pats.

3. Help the class develop body percussion for the second rhythm. For example, "ti-ti ti-ti ti-ti ti-ti" could be rubbing hands together.

4. Now, have students do the first body rhythm followed by the second.

5. Continue helping the class create body percussion motions for each rhythm. After each, go back to the beginning and repeat the previous ones learned.

6. Once the students have mastered the measures combined, do in a round.

....

Personal note: The more creative you get with the body percussion, the more the students will love this activity. I use sticking out the tongue, dropping the jaw and "slapping" the cheeks at the same time, tapping fingers on a chair, yawning, etc. This is an absolute favorite of my students and they love to enhance it by making up their own. This also introduces the idea of the class composing original pieces. FUN!

....

GROCERY LIST

Materials

• Your grocery list (seriously, that's it!)

• Pencil and paper for each student

1. Read the first item on your grocery list.

2. Have the students figure out what the rhythm would be for that item. For example, "Butterfinger" = ti-ti ti-ti, "Cool Whip" = ta ta.

3. Give the students paper and pencil and ask them to write down the ingredients for a meal they like.

4. When they are done, have them write the rhythms of each item they listed.

5. Finally, have the students pair up and ask them to play each other's "grocery lists" on a percussion instrument or by simply clapping the rhythms.

A BUNCH OF SMARTIES

Materials

- Several bags of Smarties candy (or similar round candy)
- Ice cream sticks
- Plastic baggies
- Paper for each student

To Prepare

Place several ice cream sticks in a baggie with the candy. Prepare one baggie for each student.

1. Begin by clapping rhythms using quarter and eighth notes to the class and ask them to echo back the rhythm as they rhythm speak.
2. Hand each student the prepared baggie and a piece of paper and have them spread out on the floor. Ask them to place the paper on the ground with the baggie on top.
3. Explain they are to recreate clapped rhythms by making quarter notes and eighth notes on the paper with the supplies in their baggie.
4. Clap a four-beat rhythm.
5. Students recreate it on the paper.
6. Continue this process for as long as time allows.

....

Personal note: If your resources allow, absolutely, let them eat the candy at the end of the activity!

....

BEAN BAG TOSS

Materials

- Four bean bags
- Several large squares (half of a big poster size is ideal)
- Staff paper ready to document the melodies created

To Prepare

Label each square with a different solfege name (or number) and tape these together. Place these on the floor in an open area.

1. Line students up in a row to "toss" the bean bag at the poster board.
2. After each throw, document which pitch the bag landed on. (If the bean bag lands on the square at all, the pitch found on the square is the one used.)
3. Write the pitches in order on a sheet music for the class to see.
4. Now, have the students sing the line of music that was created.
5. Discuss what sections were more difficult, which intervals were a struggle, etc.
6. Have students help "re-write" the melody to be more attractive or easier to read.

Enhancement Activity

Put the students in groups and have them create a bean bag melody together. Have the students perform their songs for each other.

BLIND DRAW

Materials

- White board or chalk board for writing
- Paper and pencil for each student (Consider small dry erase boards, if available)

1. Show the students a music symbol, for example, a "treble clef."
2. Talk about the symbol and what it means.
3. Have them watch you draw it very slowly. (The slower the better.)
4. Ask them to draw the treble clef on their paper *without* looking down to see what they are drawing. (This is called a Blind Draw.) Draw the treble clef slowly on the board as they draw.
5. Now, have them check their papers to see how they did.
6. Have them draw the symbol again, but this time while looking.
7. Continue doing this with other symbols you want them to learn.

....

Personal note: This is a lot of fun. I use this with crescendo, decrescendo, treble clef, bass clef and sforzando. They can quickly point the symbols out in music we are doing in class after we have done this activity.

....

POST-IT MELODY

Materials

- Post-it® notes, enough for each student to receive two
- Pencil for each student
- Music staff visual on which to notate

1. Give each student two Post-it notes and tell them to pick any two pitches, for example "low Do" and "high Do."
2. Have them write these pitches on *one* of the Post-it notes.
3. Now, ask them to either draw a quarter note, half note or a pair of 8th notes on the other note.
4. One at a time, have the students bring their Post-it notes to you.
5. Pair the pitch with the rhythm that was given and write this on the music staff for all to see.
6. Have the class determine where the measure lines should be placed.
7. Finally, have them sight read the line of music that was created.

Enhancement Activity

Once this is written by the class, you can now use it to do "Meet in the Middle" (pg. 40), "Sing on Sight in Rounds" (pg. 37), or other activities in this book.

SOUND STORIES

Materials

- Paper and pencil for groups
- Unpitched instruments (conventional or non-conventional)

To Prepare

Write a story on a visual. Keep it short and simple. For example,

> "A man was standing at the busy street corner. He saw a young boy on a bicycle ride by. There was an old woman with a cane crossing the street. He heard a fire truck in the distance. A policeman blew his whistle for all to pass. The man went on his way."

1. Have the students read the board story aloud.

2. Ask them to think of an instrument that can be played at the end of each sentence. Explain this instrument will play at the end of this sentence when the story is re-read.

3. Divide your class into small groups of 6-8 students. Explain they will work in teams to write their own sound story. They will need to include an instrument sound for each sentence.

4. Give them these guidelines:

   - There must be a location or an event.

   - It must also be five sentences in length.

5. At the end of class or when they are ready, have them take turns reading and performing their sound stories.

....

Personal note: This is **not** a short activity. It generally takes my students a class period to accomplish this. They enjoy the ownership of writing their own story. The room gets a little "rowdy" when they are practicing, so I give a time to practice, call time and then 5 minutes to finish.

....

JINGLE WRITING

Materials

- Advertising pages from a magazine or from the Internet (For reuse, consider laminating.) You will need enough to give one to each group.
- Pencil and paper for each group

1. Have students help you brainstorm a list of kids' songs. For example,
   - "Mary Had a Little Lamb"
   - "The Wheels on the Bus"
   - "Itsy Bitsy Spider" (etc.)

2. Tell them they are going to write new lyrics to a common childhood song and make it into a jingle that is designed to make people want to buy the item from the advertisement.

3. Divide the students into manageable small groups (6-8) and give each a paper/pencil and an advertising page.

4. Give the students a time limit on creating their jingle. (8-10 minutes)

5. Allow a five-minute practice time for students to sing through their jingles together as a group.

6. Have students perform their jingles for each other.

Extension Activity

Once students understand this activity, do it again another day, but give them a new product and tell them they have to, not only make up the tune they will use, but they are to also add small amounts of choreography. Film them, if you can.

Personal note: When I film the class performances, I put them into a DVD movie and play it before their concert when the parents are finding their seats.

SOLVE THE PROBLEM

Material

- Pencil for each student

To Prepare

On a piece of staff paper, create lines of music that contain rhythm errors. (Each line should have an error in it.) Make enough copies of this paper to give to each student.

1. Hand out the music sheets to the class and ask them to sight sing the first line together.
2. Next, have the students search for the mistakes found in that music line.
3. Ask them to correct the mistakes with their pencils.
4. Sight sing through the second line.
5. Repeat steps 3 above.
6. Continue doing until the page is completed.

Enhancement Activity

Give the students lines of music that are written *correctly*. Have them listen to you sing them while they mark the errors *you* make with a pencil. This provides an excellent ear training and music reading exercise into one activity.

Personal note: This is a part of the analytical process of music. It is important that students are able to edit and look through for errors. This makes them able to foresee problems in the literature they are singing in class.

TIE TIME

Materials

- Several long and wide ribbons. (These need to be long enough to tie around the wrists of two students with some slack in between.)
- Dry erase marker and eraser

To Prepare

On a large piece of paper, write the number of quarter notes that would match students on a team and laminate. (For example, if you divide your students into three teams and each team has eight members, you will need to write eight quarter notes on the paper.)

1. Divide students into teams. Depending on your class size, 8-12 players work well.

2. Using the dry erase marker, draw a tie on the laminated paper between any of the quarter notes found there.

3. Review what a tie and how it "ties" two notes together. While explaining, demonstrate how it works by selecting two students and tying them together at the wrists with one of the ribbons. Show them how their bodies represent the quarter notes and the ribbon, the tie.

4. Explain you will be writing a new rhythm on the paper by using a tie and they must work as a team to tie the correct "notes" together to recreate what is shown.

5. Erase the marker from your example and tie two different quarters together. Show this to the teams and say "GO!"

6. The team that recreates the rhythm first gets a point.

7. Continue to do this by erasing and redrawing the tie until all the combinations of ties have been exhausted.

Personal note: To help control this lesson, suggest that each team select the two members who will be "tied notes." Have these students tie their wrists together. Then, as the new rhythm is given, these members can move themselves accordingly. Another suggestion is to have all of the teams decide on a permanent standing order (maybe alphabetical) for their members. When the new rhythm is given, the ribbon is passed to the appropriate couple that, in turn, ties their wrists together to create the correct rhythm.

About the Writers

CRISTI CARY MILLER

Cristi Miller is highly regarded across the United States as a master teacher, conductor and composer. After graduating from Oklahoma State University, she began her teaching career instructing grades 7-12. She eventually moved to the Putnam City School system in 1989 where she worked in the elementary classroom for 21 years. In 1992, Mrs. Miller was selected as the Putnam City Teacher of the Year and in 1998 received one of the four "Excellence in Education" awards given through the Putnam City Foundation. In 2008, she became a National Board Certified Teacher and in 2009, she was selected as the Putnam City PTA Teacher of the Year. Recently, Mrs. Miller became a part of the Fine Arts Staff at Heritage Hall Schools in the Oklahoma City area where she teaches middle school music. Cristi has served as the Elementary Representative on the Oklahoma Choral Directors Association Board of Directors as well as the Elementary Vice President and President for the Oklahoma Music Educators Association. Along with her teaching responsibilities, Cristi authors and co-authors a column for a national music magazine entitled *Music Express* and was a contributing writer for the Macmillan McGraw-Hill music textbook series, *Spotlight on Music*. In addition, she serves as the consulting editor for *Little Schoolhouse* book series, "Christopher Kazoo and Bongo Boo." Mrs. Miller is frequently in demand as a clinician and director across the United States and Canada with numerous choral pieces and books in publication through Hal Leonard Corporation. She has also been the recipient of several ASCAP awards for her music. Cristi and her husband, Rick, live in Oklahoma City.

ANGELA K. MCKENNA

Angela McKenna is a choral music educator that resides in Edmond, Oklahoma. She has spent her career working with a large choral program that consistently is awarded superior ratings, top prizes and sweepstakes at choral and show choir contests. She is a member of ACDA, OMEA and several regional choral conductor organizations. She received her Bachelor's of Music Education from the University of Central Oklahoma. She is frequently used as a conductor for honor choirs and festivals across the state of Oklahoma and enjoys getting to work with students of all ages. She is the founder of the Young Voices of Edmond's Broadway Tonight Choir at the University of Central Oklahoma.

TEACHER NOTES